HOW TO MASTER HEALTHY HABITS

Build A Strong Foundation for Health, Boost Productivity, Sustain Growth and Development, and Transform Your Life.

PRADIP DAS

© Copyright 2024 - All rights reserved.

The content contained within this book may not be reproduced, duplicated, or transmitted without direct written permission from the author or the publisher. Under no circumstances will any blame or legal responsibility be held against the publisher, or author, for any damages, reparation, or monetary loss due to the information contained within this book. Either directly or indirectly.

Legal Notice:

This book is copyright protected. This book is only for personal use. You cannot amend, distribute, sell, use, quote or paraphrase any part, or the content within this book, without the consent of the author or publisher.

Disclaimer Notice:

Please note the information contained within this document is for educational and entertainment purposes only. All effort has been executed to present accurate, up to date, and reliable, complete information. No warranties of any kind are declared or implied. Readers acknowledge that the author is not engaging in the rendering of legal, financial, medical or professional advice. The content within this book has been derived from various sources. Please consult a licensed professional before attempting any techniques outlined in this book.

By reading this document, the reader agrees that under no circumstances is the author responsible for any losses, direct or indirect, which are incurred as a result of the use of information contained within this document, including, but not limited to, — errors, omissions, or inaccuracies.

*Please scan for the other books of the **"Life Mastery"** Series.*

Table of Contents

Table of Contents 4

About The Book 5

Introduction 7

Understanding Healthy Habits 9

Building a Foundation for Success 24

Nurturing Physical Health 41

Fostering Emotional and Mental Wellness 57

Sustaining Healthy Habits for the Long Term .. 77

About The Book

In a world full of changing health trends, "How to Master Healthy Habits" presents a new way to achieve long-lasting wellness by focusing on building good habits. This book, written with clear language and understanding, shows you how to improve your health and well-being from within, with compassion and insight into human behavior.

This book takes you on a journey of self-discovery, empowering you to break free from the unhealthy habit zone. Through practical strategies and actionable advice, you'll learn how to cultivate healthy habits that stick, enabling you to thrive physically, mentally, and emotionally.

Whether you are looking to lose weight, increase energy levels, reduce stress, or simply live a more vibrant life, this book provides you with the tools, insights, and support you need to succeed. From setting meaningful goals and overcoming obstacles to creating a supportive environment and staying consistent for the long haul, "How to Master Healthy

Habits" equips you with everything you need to embark on your journey towards optimal health and well-being.

This book offers a roadmap to sustainable transformation, one habit at a time. With its practical wisdom, stories, and transformation approach, "How to Master Healthy Habits" is not just a book—it's your trusted companion on the path to lifelong wellness. So why wait? Start your journey today and discover the transformative power of healthy habits.

Introduction

Jeanne Calment was a French supercentenarian who holds the record for the longest confirmed human lifespan, living to the age of 122 years and 164 days. She was born on February 21, 1875, and passed away on August 4, 1997.

Jeanne Calment's remarkable longevity has fascinated the world, sparking curiosity about the secrets to her exceptional lifespan. While there's no single explanation for her longevity, several factors likely contributed to her remarkable health and vitality. One key factor was her adherence to a balanced and nutritious diet. Throughout her life, Calment reportedly consumed plenty of olive oil, a hallmark of the Mediterranean diet known for its numerous health benefits.

In addition to her healthy eating habits, Calment maintained an active lifestyle well into her later years. She was an enthusiastic cyclist and continued riding her bike until she reached the remarkable age of 100. Regular physical activity likely played a significant role in preserving her overall health and vitality. Equally important was Calment's positive outlook on life. Renowned for her optimistic and resilient attitude, she approached challenges with humor and grace.

Furthermore, Calment remained socially engaged throughout her life, surrounding herself with friends and family. Strong social connections have been linked to better health outcomes and increased longevity, highlighting the importance of maintaining meaningful relationships. While genetics may have played a role, Jeanne Calment's commitment to a healthy lifestyle, positive mindset, and social engagement likely contributed to her remarkable longevity, serving as an inspiration for generations to come.

We draw inspiration from Jeanne Calment's remarkable journey which teaches us that optimism, healthy habits, and social connections can contribute to a long and fulfilling life. Let's resolve to cultivate healthy habits.

Understanding Healthy Habits

Healthy habits are like small seeds that, when nurtured and cultivated, blossom into the garden of well-being. They are the daily choices and routines that contribute to our physical, mental, and emotional health, helping us live our best lives with vitality and joy. In this section, we'll explore what healthy habits are and why they're essential for our overall well-being.

Healthy habits are actions, behaviors, and choices that promote our health and well-being. They encompass a wide range of activities, from eating nutritious foods and exercising regularly to managing stress and getting enough sleep. Healthy habits are not just about what we do, but also how we do it—approaching life with mindfulness, intentionality, and self-care.

Let's take a closer look at some common examples of healthy habits:

Eating a Balanced Diet: Consuming a variety of nutrient-rich foods, including fruits, vegetables, whole grains, lean proteins, and healthy fats, to nourish our bodies and support optimal health.

Exercising Regularly: Engaging in physical activity that gets our heart pumping and our muscles moving, such as walking, jogging, swimming, or dancing, to strengthen our bodies and improve our fitness levels.

Getting Adequate Sleep: Prioritizing rest and relaxation by ensuring we get enough sleep each night, typically 7-9 hours for adults, to support physical recovery, cognitive function, and overall well-being.

Managing Stress: Implementing stress management techniques, such as deep breathing, meditation, yoga, or journaling, to reduce the negative effects of stress on our bodies and minds.

Practicing Mindfulness: Cultivating present-moment awareness and non-judgmental acceptance of our thoughts, feelings, and experiences, to enhance our mental clarity, emotional resilience, and overall sense of well-being.

Maintaining Hydration: Drinking plenty of water throughout the day to stay hydrated and support essential bodily functions, such as digestion, circulation, and temperature regulation.

Limiting Screen Time: Setting boundaries around our digital device usage, such as smartphones, computers, and televisions, to minimize distractions, reduce eye strain, and promote real-world connections.

Connecting with Others: Nurturing meaningful relationships with family, friends, and community members through regular communication, social activities, and acts of kindness, to foster a sense of belonging and support.

Practicing Gratitude: Cultivating an attitude of gratitude by acknowledging and appreciating the blessings, joys, and opportunities present in our lives, to promote positive emotions and overall life satisfaction.

Why Are Healthy Habits Essential?

Healthy habits are essential for our overall health and well-being for several reasons:

Physical Health: Healthy habits help us maintain a healthy weight, reduce the risk of chronic diseases, such as heart disease, diabetes, and cancer, and improve our overall physical fitness and vitality.

Mental Health: Healthy habits support our mental well-being by reducing stress, anxiety, and depression, enhancing cognitive function, and promoting positive emotions, resilience, and self-esteem.

Emotional Health: Healthy habits contribute to our emotional resilience and stability by helping us regulate our emotions, cope with challenges, and cultivate a sense of purpose, fulfillment, and inner peace.

Social Health: Healthy habits strengthen our social connections and support networks, fostering a sense of belonging, acceptance, and support, and reducing feelings of loneliness and isolation.

Healthy habits are the cornerstone of a vibrant and fulfilling life. By embracing habits that nourish our bodies, minds, and spirits, we can enhance our quality of life, increase our resilience to stress and adversity, and cultivate a lasting sense of well-being and happiness. So why wait? Start incorporating healthy habits into your daily routine today and reap the benefits for years to come.

The Importance of Healthy Habits

In our fast-paced world filled with endless distractions and demands, taking care of our health often takes a backseat to other priorities. Yet, the truth is that our health is the foundation upon which everything else in our lives rests. Without it, we cannot fully enjoy life's blessings or pursue our dreams and aspirations.

Healthy habits play a crucial role in maintaining and enhancing our overall well-being, enabling us to live life to the fullest and achieve our goals. In this section, we will explore the importance of healthy habits and why they are essential for a thriving, fulfilling life.

Physical Health: Healthy habits are key to maintaining good physical health. Regular exercise, nutritious eating, adequate sleep, and proper hygiene all contribute to a strong and resilient body. By adopting these habits, we can reduce the risk of chronic diseases, such as heart disease, diabetes, and obesity, and enjoy better overall health and vitality.

Mental Health: Our mental well-being is closely linked to our habits and lifestyle choices. Engaging in activities that promote mental wellness, such as practicing mindfulness, managing stress effectively, and seeking social support, can help us cope with life's challenges and maintain a positive outlook. Healthy habits can also improve cognitive function, enhance focus and concentration, and boost mood and emotional resilience.

Emotional Well-Being: Healthy habits contribute to emotional well-being by providing us with the tools and resources to manage our emotions effectively. Engaging in activities that promote self-care, such as spending time with loved ones, pursuing hobbies, and engaging in creative expression, can help us cultivate a sense of fulfillment, joy, and inner peace.

Energy and Vitality: Healthy habits are essential for maintaining energy levels and vitality throughout the day. By prioritizing activities that nourish our bodies and minds, such as eating nutritious foods, staying hydrated, and getting enough rest, we can feel more energized, focused, and productive in our daily lives.

Longevity and Quality of Life: Adopting healthy habits can significantly impact our longevity and quality of life. Research has shown that individuals who engage in regular exercise, maintain a healthy weight, and follow a balanced diet tend to live longer and enjoy a higher quality of life in their later years. By investing in our health today, we can set ourselves up for a vibrant and fulfilling future.

Role Modeling: As individuals, we have the power to influence those around us through our actions and behaviors. By embracing healthy habits and modeling positive lifestyle choices, we can inspire others to do the same, creating a ripple effect of health and wellness within our families, communities, and beyond.

Healthy habits are the cornerstone of a thriving, fulfilling life. By prioritizing our physical, mental, and emotional well-being and adopting habits that support our health goals, we can unlock our full potential and live life to the fullest. So let us embrace the power of healthy habits and take proactive steps towards a healthier, happier future.

The Science Behind Habit Formation

In our daily lives, we often find ourselves engaging in various habits—some good, some not so good. But have you ever wondered why we do the things we do, and how habits are formed in the first place? In this chapter, we'll explore the fascinating science behind habit formation, shedding light on the intricate processes that shape our behavior and offering insights into how we can harness this knowledge to cultivate healthy habits that stick.

At its core, habit formation is rooted in the complex interplay between our brains, behaviors, and environments. To understand how habits are formed, it's helpful to break down the process into three key components: the cue, the routine, and the reward.

The Trigger That Starts It All

Every habit begins with a cue—a trigger that signals to our brains that it's time to engage in a particular behavior. Cues can take many forms, ranging from external stimuli like sights, sounds, and smells to internal cues like emotions, thoughts, and physical sensations. For example, the smell of freshly brewed coffee may serve as a cue to reach for a cup, or feeling stressed may trigger the urge to bite your nails.

Understanding the role of cues in habit formation is essential because it allows us to identify the triggers that prompt our behaviors. By becoming more aware of our cues, we can take proactive steps to modify our environment and routines, making it easier to establish healthier habits.

The Behavior That Follows

Once a cue is detected, our brains automatically initiate a behavioral routine—the action or series of actions that we perform in response to the cue. These routines are often repetitive and can become deeply ingrained over time, making them feel automatic and effortless. For example, hitting the snooze button upon waking up may be part of your morning routine, or reaching for a cup of coffee when feeling tired may be a habitual response.

Understanding the role of routines in habit formation is crucial because it allows us to recognize the patterns of behavior that drive our habits. By consciously evaluating our routines and their impact on our well-being, we can begin to make intentional choices that support our health and happiness.

The Reinforcement That Keeps Us Coming Back

The final component of habit formation is the reward—the positive reinforcement that we receive for engaging in a particular behavior. Rewards can take many forms, including physical sensations like pleasure or relief, emotional benefits like stress reduction or feelings of accomplishment, or social rewards like approval or acceptance from others. For example, the feeling of satisfaction that comes from completing a workout may serve as a reward for exercising regularly, or the sense of calm that accompanies a mindfulness practice may reinforce the habit of meditating daily.

Understanding the role of rewards in habit formation is essential because it allows us to leverage the power of positive reinforcement to solidify healthy habits. By identifying the rewards that drive our behaviors, we can consciously design our environments and routines to maximize positive outcomes and minimize negative influences.

But what happens when our habits deviate, leading us down paths of unhealthy behavior? Understanding the science behind habit formation provides us with valuable insights into how we can break free from destructive patterns and cultivate new habits that align with our goals and values.

By recognizing the cues that trigger our behaviors, experimenting with new routines, and identifying the rewards that truly matter to us, we can rewire our brains and establish healthier habits that support our overall well-being.

Common Challenges in Adopting Healthy Habits

Embarking on a journey to adopt healthy habits is an admirable endeavor, but it's not without its challenges. Understanding and overcoming these obstacles is essential for success. Here, we explore some of the common challenges you may encounter along the way:

Lack of Motivation: One of the biggest hurdles in adopting healthy habits is finding the motivation to get started. It's easy to feel overwhelmed or demotivated, especially if you've tried and failed in the past. However, understanding your reasons for wanting to change and setting meaningful goals can help reignite your motivation.

Unrealistic Expectations: Many people expect instant results when adopting healthy habits, only to be disappointed when progress is slow or inconsistent. It's important to set realistic expectations and understand that change takes time. Celebrate small victories along the way and be patient with yourself.

Limited Time and Resources: Busy schedules, financial constraints, and other responsibilities can make it challenging to prioritize healthy habits. However, with careful planning and creative solutions, you can find ways to integrate healthy practices into your daily routine. Start small and gradually build upon your efforts over time.

Social Pressure and Temptations: Peer pressure, social norms, and cultural influences can make it difficult to stick to healthy habits, especially in environments where unhealthy behaviors are prevalent. Surrounding yourself with supportive friends and family members, setting boundaries, and finding alternative social activities can help you stay on track.

Emotional Eating and Stress: Many people turn to food for comfort or stress relief, leading to unhealthy eating habits and emotional imbalances. Learning to recognize and address emotional triggers, practicing mindfulness and stress management techniques, and finding healthier ways to cope with emotions can help break the cycle of emotional eating.

Lack of Knowledge and Education: Without a solid understanding of nutrition, exercise, and other aspects of health, it can be challenging to make informed decisions and adopt sustainable habits. Investing time in educating yourself, seeking guidance from experts, and experimenting with different approaches can help you build a foundation of knowledge to support your journey.

Self-Doubt and Negative Self-Talk: Negative self-talk and self-doubt can undermine your confidence and sabotage your efforts to adopt healthy habits. Cultivating self-compassion, practicing positive affirmations, and surrounding yourself with uplifting influences can help shift your mindset and build resilience in the face of adversity.

Perfectionism and All-or-Nothing Thinking: Striving for perfection and adopting an all-or-nothing mindset can set you up for failure and disappointment. Instead, focus on progress over perfection, embrace flexibility and adaptability, and celebrate the small steps you take towards your goals.

Lack of Accountability and Support: Trying to adopt healthy habits alone can be challenging, especially without accountability and support. Finding a workout buddy, joining a community or support group, or working with a coach or mentor can provide the encouragement and guidance you need to stay motivated and accountable.

Fear of Failure: Fear of failure can paralyze you and prevent you from taking action towards adopting healthy habits. However, failure is a natural part of the learning process and an opportunity for growth. Embrace setbacks as learning experiences, adjust your approach as needed, and keep moving forward with determination and resilience.

If you are able to recognize and address these common challenges, you can overcome obstacles and pave the way for success on your journey to adopting healthy habits. Progress is not always linear, and setbacks are an inevitable part of the process. Stay committed, stay resilient, and keep moving forward towards a healthier, happier you.

Building a Foundation for Success

Building a foundation for success is essential. Setting goals is one of the primary requirements. Setting goals for healthy living is like charting a course for a journey. Just like you need a map to reach your destination, setting clear goals helps you navigate your path to better health and well-being.

Why Set Goals?

Imagine you're planning a road trip. Without a destination in mind, you might end up wandering aimlessly, unsure of where you're going or how to get there. Goals serve as your destination—they give you direction, focus, and motivation to keep moving forward, even when the journey gets tough.

When it comes to healthy living, goals help you clarify what you want to achieve and why it's important to you. Whether your goal is to lose weight, improve your fitness, or reduce stress, setting clear objectives helps you stay motivated and committed to making positive changes in your life.

How to Set Goals Effectively

Setting goals effectively involves more than just picking a target and hoping for the best. It requires thoughtful planning, realistic expectations, and a willingness to adapt as you progress. Here are some steps to help you set goals that are achievable and sustainable:

Identify Your Why: Start by asking yourself why you want to improve your health. What motivates you? What are the benefits of reaching your goals? Understanding your reasons for wanting to change will help you stay committed when challenges arise.

Be Specific: Instead of setting vague goals like "I want to get healthier," be specific about what you want to achieve. For example, you might set a goal to exercise for 30 minutes, five days a week, or to eat five servings of fruits and vegetables every day.

Make Them Measurable: A goal should be something you can measure so that you can track your progress.

Whether it's tracking your daily steps, monitoring your food intake, or recording your workouts, having concrete data helps you see how you're doing and make adjustments as needed.

Set Realistic Expectations: While it's important to challenge yourself, be realistic about what you can achieve. Setting overly ambitious goals can lead to frustration and burnout. Start with small, attainable steps, and gradually increase the difficulty as you build momentum.

Break Them Down: Break your larger goals into smaller, more manageable tasks. This makes them less overwhelming and allows you to focus on making progress one step at a time. Celebrate each milestone along the way to stay motivated.

Write Them Down: Research shows that people who write down their goals are more likely to achieve them. Write your goals down and keep them somewhere visible, like on your fridge or bathroom mirror, to serve as a daily reminder of what you're working towards.

Create a Plan: Once you've set your goals, create a plan for how you'll achieve them. Identify potential obstacles and brainstorm strategies for overcoming them. Having a roadmap will help you stay focused and accountable.

Tips for Staying on Track

Setting goals is just the first step—staying on track requires consistency, commitment, and resilience. Here are some tips to help you stay motivated and accountable:

Find Your Why: Remind yourself why you're working towards your goals and the benefits they'll bring to your life. Visualize your success and stay focused on your reasons for wanting to change.

Track Your Progress: Keep track of your progress regularly to see how far you've come and where you still need to go. Use a journal, app, or spreadsheet to record your activities, measurements, and achievements.

Stay Flexible: Be willing to adapt your goals and strategies as needed. Life is full of unexpected twists and turns, so it's important to be flexible and adjust your plans accordingly.

Seek Support: Surround yourself with supportive friends, family members, or a community of like-minded individuals who can cheer you on and provide encouragement when you need it most.

Celebrate Your Successes: Don't forget to celebrate your victories, no matter how small. Recognize and reward yourself for your hard work and progress along the way.

Setting goals for healthy living is the first step towards creating a life of vitality, happiness, and well-being. By clarifying your objectives, creating a plan, and staying committed to your journey, you can achieve remarkable results and transform your health for the better. Remember, every step you take towards your goals brings you closer to the vibrant, fulfilling life you deserve. So set your sights high, take action, and watch as your dreams become a reality.

Creating Your Personalized Health Plan

When it comes to achieving your health goals, one size does not fit all. Each person is unique, with individual needs, preferences, and challenges. That's why creating a personalized health plan is essential for success. In this chapter, we'll explore how to craft a plan that's tailored to your specific needs and goals, setting you up for long-term success on your journey to better health.

Step 1: Define Your Goals

The first step in creating your personalized health plan is to define your goals. What do you want to achieve? Whether it's losing weight, increasing energy levels, improving mental clarity, or reducing stress, clearly defining your goals will give you direction and motivation.

Take some time to reflect on what matters most to you and what you hope to achieve with your health plan. Write down your goals in specific, measurable terms. For example, instead of saying "I want to lose weight," you might say "I want to lose 10 kilograms in the next three months."

Step 2: Assess Your Current Habits

Next, take an honest look at your current habits and behaviors. What are you doing well, and what areas could use improvement? Be gentle with yourself and approach this assessment with curiosity rather than judgment.

Keep a journal for a few days to track your eating habits, exercise routine, sleep patterns, stress levels, and any other relevant factors. This will help you identify patterns and areas for improvement.

Step 3: Identify Obstacles and Challenges

Every journey to better health comes with its fair share of obstacles and challenges. Anticipating these challenges ahead of time can help you prepare for them and develop strategies to overcome them.

Think about what obstacles you might encounter on your journey, whether it's a busy schedule, emotional eating habits, lack of motivation, or social pressures. Once you've identified your obstacles, brainstorm potential solutions and strategies for overcoming them.

Step 4: Create Your Action Plan

Now that you have a clear understanding of your goals, current habits, and potential obstacles, it's time to create your action plan. This plan will outline the specific steps you'll take to achieve your goals and overcome challenges along the way.

Break down your goals into smaller, manageable tasks, and create a timeline for completing each task. Be realistic about what you can accomplish and prioritize the most important actions.

For example, if your goal is to eat healthier, your action plan might include tasks such as meal planning, grocery shopping, cooking at home more often, and finding healthier alternatives to your favorite foods.

Step 5: Implement and Adjust

With your action plan in hand, it's time to put it into action. Start by taking small, consistent steps towards your goals each day. Celebrate your successes along the way and be gentle with yourself when you encounter setbacks.

As you progress on your journey, pay attention to what's working and what's not. Be willing to adjust your plan as needed based on your experiences and feedback from your body.

Creating lasting change takes time and patience. Stay committed to your goals, stay flexible in your approach, and above all, stay kind to yourself as you navigate the ups and downs of your health journey.

By creating a personalized health plan that aligns with your goals, values, and lifestyle, you'll set yourself up for success and pave the way for a healthier, happier future. So take the first step today and start crafting your personalized health plan—you deserve it!

Overcoming Barriers to Change

Change can be hard. Whether it's adopting a healthier diet, starting an exercise routine, or breaking a bad habit, the journey towards change is often nervous with challenges and obstacles. But fear not, for overcoming these barriers is not only possible but entirely achievable with the right mindset, strategies, and support. The following are some common barriers to change and learn how to overcome them with practical tips and insights.

Identifying Barriers: The first step in overcoming barriers to change is recognizing them for what they are. Common barriers include fear of failure, lack of motivation, self-doubt, and resistance to change. By acknowledging these barriers, you can begin to address them head-on and develop strategies to overcome them.

Setting Realistic Goals: One of the biggest barriers to change is setting unrealistic goals. When goals are too lofty or unattainable, it's easy to become discouraged and give up altogether. Instead, set small, achievable goals that you can celebrate along the way. Break larger goals into smaller, manageable steps, and focus on progress rather than perfection.

Cultivating Self-Compassion: Change is hard, and setbacks are inevitable. Instead of beating yourself up over perceived failures, practice self-compassion and kindness towards yourself. Remember that change is a journey, not a destination, and be patient with yourself as you navigate the ups and downs along the way.

Building a Support System: Surround yourself with people who believe in you and support your goals. Whether it's friends, family members, or a support group, having a strong support system can make all the difference in staying motivated and accountable. Lean on your support system for encouragement, advice, and guidance when needed.

Addressing Fear of Failure: Fear of failure is a common barrier to change, often leading to procrastination and self-sabotage. Instead of letting fear hold you back, reframe failure as an opportunity for growth and learning. Embrace the mindset of "failing forward," where setbacks become valuable lessons that propel you closer to your goals.

Cultivating Motivation: Motivation can ebb and flow, making it challenging to stay committed to change. To cultivate lasting motivation, connect with your deeper why—the reasons behind your desire for change. Whether it's improving your health, enhancing your quality of life, or setting a positive example for loved ones, tapping into your intrinsic motivations can fuel your journey towards change.

Developing Resilience: Change is rarely linear, and setbacks are par for the course. Developing resilience—the ability to bounce back from adversity—is key to overcoming barriers and staying on track. Practice resilience-building strategies such as reframing setbacks as opportunities, practicing gratitude, and focusing on your strengths and successes.

Seeking Professional Support: Sometimes, overcoming barriers to change requires professional guidance and support. Whether it's working with a therapist, coach, or healthcare provider, don't hesitate to seek help if you're struggling to make progress on your own. Professional support can provide valuable insights, accountability, and resources to help you overcome barriers and achieve your goals.

While overcoming barriers to change may not always be easy, it is entirely possible with the right mindset, strategies, and support. By identifying barriers, setting realistic goals, cultivating self-compassion, building a support system, addressing fear of failure, cultivating motivation, developing resilience, and seeking professional support when needed, you can overcome obstacles and embark on a journey of meaningful and lasting change. But, you have the power to create the life you desire—step by step, one barrier at a time.

Building Motivation and Persistence

Motivation and persistence are like the twin engines that drive us toward our goals and dreams. They give us the fuel we need to keep going when the road gets tough, and they inspire us to push through obstacles and challenges with unwavering determination. Let us know, how you can cultivate motivation and persistence to build a solid foundation for success in adopting and maintaining healthy habits.

Find Your Why: Motivation begins with a clear understanding of why you want to make a change. Take some time to reflect on your reasons for wanting to adopt healthier habits. Are you looking to improve your energy levels, lose weight, or reduce stress? Whatever your reasons may be, identifying your "why" will give you a sense of purpose and direction, making it easier to stay motivated when faced with challenges.

Set Meaningful Goals: Goals give us something to strive for and provide a roadmap for success. When setting goals for your health and well-being, make sure they are specific, measurable, achievable, relevant, and time-bound (SMART). Break larger goals down into smaller, manageable steps, and celebrate your progress along the way. This will help keep you motivated and focused on your journey.

Surround Yourself with Support: Surround yourself with people who uplift and support you on your journey toward better health. Whether it's friends, family members, or a supportive community, having a strong support system can make all the difference when it comes to staying motivated and accountable. Share your goals with others, and don't be afraid to ask for help when you need it.

Cultivate Positive Self-Talk: The way we talk to ourselves has a powerful impact on our motivation and persistence. Replace negative self-talk with positive affirmations and encouragement. Remind yourself of your strengths, successes, and progress, and don't dwell on setbacks or mistakes. By following a mindset of positivity and self-compassion, you'll be better equipped to stay motivated and resilient in the face of challenges.

Visualize Success: Visualization is a powerful tool for enhancing motivation and persistence. Take some time each day to visualize yourself achieving your goals and living the healthy, vibrant life you desire. Imagine how it will feel to reach your goals, and let that vision inspire and motivate you to keep moving forward, even when the going gets tough.

Practice Self-Care: Taking care of your physical, mental, and emotional well-being is essential for maintaining motivation and persistence. Make time for activities that nourish your body, mind, and soul, such as exercise, meditation, hobbies, and spending time with loved ones. Prioritize rest and relaxation, and listen to your body's cues for rest and rejuvenation.

Stay Flexible and Adaptive: Flexibility and adaptability are key traits of resilient individuals. Understand that setbacks and challenges are a normal part of the journey toward better health, and be willing to adjust your approach as needed. Instead of viewing obstacles as roadblocks, see them as opportunities for growth and learning. Stay open-minded and flexible in your approach, and don't be afraid to try new strategies or seek support when needed.

Celebrate Your Progress: Finally, don't forget to celebrate your progress along the way. Take time to acknowledge and celebrate each milestone and achievement, no matter how small. Whether it's losing a few pounds, sticking to your exercise routine for a week, or making healthier food choices, every step forward is worth celebrating. By recognizing and celebrating your progress, you'll reinforce your motivation and persistence, making it easier to stay committed to your goals in the long run.

Cultivating motivation and persistence is essential for building a strong foundation for success in adopting and maintaining healthy habits. By finding your why, setting meaningful goals, surrounding yourself with support, practicing positive self-talk, visualizing success, prioritizing self-care, staying flexible and adaptive, and celebrating your progress, you can stay motivated and resilient on your journey toward better health and well-being. You should always remember that small steps taken consistently over time can lead to big results, so keep moving forward with confidence and determination.

Nurturing Physical Health

Eating well is like giving your body a gift every day. Just like a car needs the right fuel to run smoothly, your body needs the right nutrients to function at its best. That's why establishing a balanced diet is so important—it's the foundation of good health and vitality.

What is a Balanced Diet?

A balanced diet is all about getting the right mix of nutrients your body needs to stay healthy. This includes carbohydrates, proteins, fats, vitamins, minerals, and water. Each nutrient plays a unique role in keeping your body running smoothly, so it's important to include a variety of foods in your diet to ensure you're getting everything you need.

Carbohydrates: These are your body's main source of energy. They come from foods like bread, pasta, rice, potatoes, and fruits. Choose whole grains and complex carbohydrates, like brown rice and whole wheat bread, for sustained energy and better overall health.

Proteins: Protein is essential for building and repairing tissues in your body. It's found in foods like meat, poultry, fish, eggs, dairy products, beans, and nuts. Aim for a mix of animal and plant-based proteins to get all the amino acids your body needs.

Fats: Contrary to popular belief, not all fats are bad for you. Healthy fats, like those found in nuts, seeds, and olive oil, are actually good for your heart and brain. Just be mindful of portion sizes and opt for unsaturated fats over saturated and trans fats.

Vitamins and Minerals: These micronutrients are like little helpers that keep your body running smoothly. They're found in a variety of foods, so eating a diverse diet is key to getting all the vitamins and minerals your body needs. Fruits, vegetables, whole grains, and lean proteins are all great sources of vitamins and minerals.

Water: Staying hydrated is crucial for good health. Water helps regulate your body temperature, transport nutrients, flush out toxins, and keep your skin looking healthy. Aim to drink at least eight glasses of water a day, and more if you're active or live in a hot climate.

Tips for Establishing a Balanced Diet

Now that you know what a balanced diet looks like, here are some tips to help you establish healthy eating habits:

Plan Ahead: Take some time each week to plan your meals and snacks. This will help you make healthier choices and avoid the temptation of grabbing fast food or unhealthy snacks when you're hungry.

Fill Up on Fruits and Vegetables: Aim to fill half your plate with fruits and vegetables at each meal. They're packed with vitamins, minerals, and fiber, and they're low in calories, so you can eat plenty of them without worrying about gaining weight.

Choose Whole Grains: Opt for whole grains like brown rice, quinoa, oats, and whole wheat bread and pasta. They're higher in fiber and nutrients than refined grains, which have been stripped of their bran and germ during processing.

Include Lean Proteins: Choose lean proteins like chicken, turkey, fish, beans, lentils, and tofu. They're lower in saturated fat and calories than fatty cuts of meat, and they're packed with nutrients your body needs to stay healthy.

Limit Added Sugars and Processed Foods: Try to limit your intake of sugary drinks, sweets, and processed foods like chips, cookies, and fast food. They're often high in calories, sugar, and unhealthy fats, and they can lead to weight gain and other health problems over time.

Listen to Your Body: Pay attention to your hunger and fullness cues, and eat when you're hungry and stop when you're full. Avoid eating out of boredom or stress, and try to eat slowly and mindfully to savor your food and prevent overeating.

Be Flexible: It's okay to indulge in your favorite foods occasionally. The key is moderation and balance, so don't beat yourself up if you slip up or indulge in a treat every now and then.

By following these tips and making small changes to your eating habits, you can establish a balanced diet that nourishes your body, fuels your activities, and supports your overall health and well-being. So why wait? Start building your plate with nutrient-rich foods today and reap the benefits of a healthy, balanced diet for years to come.

Incorporating Exercise into Your Routine

Physical activity is not just about burning calories or sculpting muscles—it's about nurturing your body, boosting your mood, and enhancing your overall well-being.

Why Exercise Matters

Exercise offers a myriad of benefits for your physical, mental, and emotional health. From strengthening your heart and bones to reducing stress and anxiety, the positive effects of regular physical activity are undeniable. Here are just a few reasons why exercise matters:

Improved Physical Health: Regular exercise can help you maintain a healthy weight, reduce your risk of chronic diseases such as heart disease and diabetes, and improve your overall fitness levels.

Enhanced Mental Well-Being: Exercise has been shown to boost mood, alleviate symptoms of depression and anxiety, and promote feelings of relaxation and well-being.

Increased Energy Levels: Engaging in physical activity can increase your energy levels, enhance your stamina, and improve your ability to perform daily tasks with ease.

Better Sleep: Regular exercise can help regulate your sleep patterns, making it easier to fall asleep, stay asleep, and wake up feeling refreshed.

Stress Relief: Exercise is a powerful stress reliever, helping to reduce levels of stress hormones in the body and promote feelings of calm and relaxation.

Incorporating Exercise into Your Daily Routine

Finding time for exercise amidst the demands of work, family, and other obligations can be challenging, but with a little creativity and determination, it's entirely possible. Here are some practical strategies for incorporating exercise into your daily routine:

Schedule It: Treat exercise like any other important appointment and schedule it into your day. Whether it's a morning jog, a lunchtime walk, or an evening yoga class, block out time on your calendar for physical activity.

Make It Fun: Choose activities that you enjoy and look forward to, whether it's dancing, swimming, hiking, or playing a sport. When exercise feels like play, you're more likely to stick with it.

Break It Up: You don't have to do all your exercise at once. Break it up into smaller chunks throughout the day—take the stairs instead of the elevator, go for short walks during your breaks, or do a quick workout during commercials while watching TV.

Get Creative: Think outside the box when it comes to exercise. Incorporate physical activity into everyday tasks, such as gardening, cleaning, or playing with your kids or pets.

Buddy Up: Find a workout buddy or join a group exercise class for added motivation and accountability. Exercising with others can make it more enjoyable and help you stay committed to your fitness goals.

Make It Convenient: Choose activities that are easy to fit into your schedule and require minimal equipment or preparation. Whether it's a home workout, a neighborhood walk, or a bike ride to work, make exercise as convenient as possible.

Set Realistic Goals: Start small and gradually build up to more challenging workouts. Set realistic goals for yourself and celebrate your progress along the way.

Listen to Your Body: Pay attention to how your body feels during and after exercise. If something doesn't feel right, adjust your intensity or take a break. Remember that rest and recovery are just as important as exercise itself.

Stay Consistent: Consistency is key when it comes to exercise. Aim for regular, consistent workouts, even if they're short or low-intensity. Building a habit of exercise over time will yield long-term benefits for your health and well-being.

Be Kind to Yourself: Remember that exercise is not about perfection—it's about progress. Be kind to yourself, celebrate your successes, and don't be too hard on yourself if you miss a workout or fall off track. Tomorrow is a new day, and every small step counts towards a healthier, happier you.

Incorporating exercise into your daily routine doesn't have to be daunting or overwhelming. By taking small, manageable steps and finding activities that you enjoy, you can reap the countless benefits of physical activity and nurture your body, mind, and spirit for years to come. So lace up those sneakers, step outside, and embrace the joy of movement—it's time to make exercise a natural and enjoyable part of your everyday life.

Prioritizing Sleep and Rest

Sleep and rest often take a backseat to our other commitments and responsibilities. However, prioritizing sleep and rest is essential for our overall health and well-being.

Why Sleep Matters

Sleep is not just a luxury—it's a biological necessity. It's during sleep that our bodies repair and regenerate, our brains consolidate memories and process emotions, and our immune systems recharge. Without enough sleep, our physical and mental health can suffer.

The Impact of Sleep on Physical Health

Getting enough sleep is crucial for maintaining optimal physical health. Sleep deprivation has been linked to a range of health problems, including obesity, diabetes, heart disease, and weakened immune function. Additionally, lack of sleep can impair cognitive function, increase the risk of accidents and injuries, and contribute to mood disorders such as anxiety and depression.

Tips for Better Sleep and Rest

Establish a Consistent Sleep Schedule: Go to bed and wake up at the same time every day, even on weekends. This helps regulate your body's internal clock and promotes better sleep quality.

Create a Relaxing Bedtime Routine: Develop a soothing bedtime routine to signal to your body that it's time to wind down. This could include activities such as reading, taking a warm bath, or practicing relaxation techniques like deep breathing or meditation.

Create a Comfortable Sleep Environment: Make sure your bedroom is conducive to sleep by keeping it cool, dark, and quiet. Invest in a comfortable mattress and pillows, and consider using blackout curtains or white noise machines to block out distractions.

Limit Screen Time Before Bed: The blue light emitted by screens can disrupt your body's natural sleep-wake cycle, making it harder to fall asleep. Try to limit screen time in the hour before bed, and consider using apps or settings that reduce blue light exposure.

Watch Your Caffeine and Alcohol Intake: Avoid consuming caffeine or alcohol close to bedtime, as both can interfere with sleep. Instead, opt for non-caffeinated beverages like herbal tea or warm milk to help you relax before bed.

Exercise Regularly: Regular physical activity can improve sleep quality and duration, so aim to incorporate exercise into your daily routine. Just make sure to avoid vigorous exercise close to bedtime, as it can be stimulating and make it harder to fall asleep.

Manage Stress: Chronic stress can disrupt sleep patterns and contribute to sleep problems. Practice stress management techniques such as mindfulness, yoga, or journaling to help calm your mind and relax your body before bed.

Limit Naps: While short naps can be beneficial for some people, long or irregular napping during the day can interfere with nighttime sleep. If you need to nap, aim for a short nap of 20-30 minutes early in the day.

Seek Professional Help if Needed: If you consistently struggle with sleep problems despite trying these tips, consider seeking help from a healthcare professional. They can help identify underlying issues and provide personalized recommendations for improving your sleep.

Prioritizing sleep and rest is essential for our physical health and well-being. By making sleep a priority, establishing healthy sleep habits, and creating a conducive sleep environment, we can improve our sleep quality and enjoy the many benefits of a good night's rest. So tonight, let's commit to giving our bodies the rest and rejuvenation they need to thrive.

Managing Stress and Mental Well-Being

Stress has become an all too familiar companion nowadays, often present around every corner, ready to attack when we least expect it. But while stress may be a natural part of life, learning how to manage it effectively is essential for our overall health and well-being.

Understanding Stress:

Stress is our body's natural response to perceived threats or challenges, triggering a cascade of physiological and psychological reactions designed to help us cope with danger. However, when stress becomes chronic or overwhelming, it can take a toll on our physical, mental, and emotional health.

Recognizing the Signs of Stress:

It's important to recognize the signs of stress so that we can address them before they escalate. Common symptoms of stress include:

Physical symptoms: such as headaches, muscle tension, fatigue, and digestive issues.

Emotional symptoms: such as irritability, anxiety, depression, and mood swings.

Cognitive symptoms: such as racing thoughts, difficulty concentrating, and memory problems.

Behavioral symptoms: such as changes in appetite, sleep disturbances, and withdrawal from social activities.

Coping Strategies for Stress Management:

Fortunately, there are many effective strategies for managing stress and promoting mental well-being. Here are some simple yet powerful techniques to help you cope with stress:

Deep Breathing: Practice deep breathing exercises to activate the body's relaxation response and calm the mind.

Mindfulness Meditation: Engage in mindfulness meditation to cultivate present moment awareness and reduce stress levels.

Physical Activity: Incorporate regular exercise into your routine to release tension, boost mood, and improve overall well-being.

Healthy Lifestyle Habits: Maintain a balanced diet, get adequate sleep, and avoid excessive alcohol, caffeine, and nicotine, as these can exacerbate stress.

Time Management: Prioritize tasks, set realistic goals, and delegate responsibilities to avoid feeling overwhelmed.

Social Support: Lean on friends, family members, or support groups for emotional support and encouragement during stressful times.

Positive Coping Skills: Develop healthy coping mechanisms such as journaling, practicing gratitude, engaging in hobbies, or seeking professional help when needed.

Seeking Professional Help:

If stress becomes overwhelming or begins to interfere with your daily life, don't hesitate to seek professional help. A qualified mental health professional can provide guidance, support, and resources to help you manage stress and improve your mental well-being.

Managing stress is not about eliminating it altogether but rather learning how to face life's challenges with resilience, grace, and self-care. By incorporating these strategies into your daily routine, you can cultivate greater peace of mind, enhance your overall well-being, and embrace life with renewed vitality and resilience.

Please check the Book Series of
"The Art of Living"

Fostering Emotional and Mental Wellness

Building and nurturing positive relationships is essential for our emotional and mental well-being. When we have strong connections with others, we feel supported, understood, and valued, which can significantly impact our overall happiness and resilience.

Why Positive Relationships Matter

Positive relationships are like sunshine for the soul—they brighten our days, lift our spirits, and provide us with a sense of belonging and connection. Research has shown that people who have strong, supportive relationships with friends, family, and community tend to be happier, healthier, and more resilient in the face of life's challenges.

When we have positive relationships in our lives, we experience a range of benefits for our emotional and mental well-being:

Emotional Support: Positive relationships provide us with a safe space to express our thoughts, feelings, and vulnerabilities without fear of judgment. Having someone to confide in during difficult times can help us cope with stress and reduce feelings of loneliness and isolation.

Sense of Belonging: Positive relationships foster a sense of belonging and connection to others, which is essential for our mental health. When we feel connected to a community or social group, we're more likely to experience feelings of happiness, fulfillment, and purpose in life.

Increased Resilience: Having supportive relationships can bolster our resilience and ability to bounce back from adversity. Knowing that we have a network of friends and loved ones who have our back can give us the strength and courage to face life's challenges with confidence.

Improved Self-Esteem: Positive relationships contribute to our sense of self-worth and self-esteem. When we receive love, acceptance, and validation from others, we're more likely to see ourselves in a positive light and feel confident in our abilities.

Better Mental Health: Strong relationships have been linked to lower rates of depression, anxiety, and other mental health issues. The social support and companionship provided by positive relationships can buffer against the negative effects of stress and contribute to overall emotional well-being.

Practical Tips for Cultivating Positive Relationships

Now that we understand the importance of positive relationships for emotional and mental wellness, let's explore some practical tips for building and nurturing meaningful connections with others:

Prioritize Quality Over Quantity: Focus on cultivating a few close, meaningful relationships rather than spreading yourself too thin. Invest time and energy in nurturing deep connections with friends, family members, or romantic partners who uplift and support you.

Be Present and Engaged: Practice active listening and genuine empathy when interacting with others. Show interest in their thoughts, feelings, and experiences, and validate their emotions without judgment. Being fully present in your interactions can strengthen your relationships and foster deeper connections.

Communicate Openly and Honestly: Maintain open and honest communication with the people in your life, sharing your thoughts, feelings, and needs openly and respectfully. Encourage others to do the same by creating a safe and supportive environment for open dialogue and expression.

Show Appreciation and Gratitude: Express gratitude and appreciation for the people who enrich your life. Take time to acknowledge their contributions, kindness, and support, whether through words of thanks, acts of kindness, or thoughtful gestures of appreciation.

Resolve Conflicts Constructively: Conflict is a natural part of any relationship, but how we handle it can either strengthen or weaken our connections with others. Approach conflicts with an open mind, a willingness to listen, and a commitment to finding mutually satisfactory solutions. Practice active listening, empathy, and compromise to resolve conflicts constructively and strengthen your relationships.

Spend Quality Time Together: Make time for shared activities and experiences that bring you closer together. Whether it's enjoying a meal together, going for a walk, or pursuing a shared hobby or interest, prioritize quality time spent in each other's company.

Set Boundaries: Establish clear boundaries in your relationships to ensure mutual respect, understanding, and autonomy. Communicate your needs, preferences, and limits openly and assertively, and respect the boundaries set by others.

Practice Forgiveness and Letting Go: Let go of grudges, resentments, and past grievances that can poison your relationships and hinder your emotional well-being. Practice forgiveness, compassion, and understanding, both towards yourself and others, and focus on moving forward with a sense of peace and acceptance.

Seek Support When Needed: Reach out for support from trusted friends, family members, or mental health professionals when facing challenges or experiencing emotional distress. Don't hesitate to lean on your support network for encouragement, guidance, and comfort during difficult times.

Cultivate Self-Compassion: Finally, remember to extend the same kindness, compassion, and understanding to yourself that you offer to others. Practice self-care, self-compassion, and self-acceptance as essential components of your overall well-being.

By implementing these practical tips and strategies, you can cultivate positive relationships that nourish your emotional and mental well-being, enrich your life, and contribute to your overall happiness and fulfillment. Building meaningful connections takes time, effort, and vulnerability, but the rewards are well worth the investment. Here's to cultivating positive relationships and fostering emotional and mental wellness in your life!

Practicing Mindfulness and Meditation

It is easy to feel overwhelmed, stressed, and disconnected from ourselves because of constant distractions and demands. But amidst the chaos of modern life, there exists a powerful antidote—a practice that has been embraced by ancient cultures for centuries and is now gaining recognition in the Western world: mindfulness and meditation.

What is Mindfulness?

At its core, mindfulness is the practice of paying attention to the present moment with openness, curiosity, and acceptance. It involves tuning into our thoughts, feelings, sensations, and surroundings without judgment, allowing us to cultivate a deeper awareness of our inner experiences and the world around us.

Mindfulness invites us to become fully present in each moment, whether we're savoring the taste of our morning coffee, feeling the warmth of the sun on our skin, or simply noticing the rhythm of our breath. By bringing our attention to the here and now, mindfulness helps us break free from the grip of rumination, worry, and stress, allowing us to experience greater peace, clarity, and contentment in our lives.

How to Practice Mindfulness

Practicing mindfulness doesn't require any special equipment or training—it's simply about bringing a sense of awareness and intentionality to our everyday activities. Here are some simple ways to incorporate mindfulness into your daily routine:

Mindful Breathing: Take a few moments to focus on your breath, noticing the rise and fall of your chest with each inhale and exhale. Allow your breath to anchor you in the present moment, guiding you back to a place of calm and centeredness whenever you feel overwhelmed or distracted.

Body Scan Meditation: Lie down or sit comfortably and bring your attention to different parts of your body, starting from your toes and gradually moving up to your head. Notice any sensations, tension, or discomfort without trying to change anything, simply observing with curiosity and kindness.

Mindful Eating: Slow down and savor each bite of your meals, paying attention to the colors, textures, and flavors of the food. Chew slowly, noticing the sensations in your mouth and the act of swallowing. Eating mindfully can help you cultivate a deeper appreciation for the nourishment your food provides and prevent overeating.

Mindful Walking: Take a leisurely stroll outdoors and pay attention to the sensations of walking—the feeling of your feet touching the ground, the movement of your body, and the sights and sounds around you. Allow yourself to be fully present in the experience, letting go of any distractions or worries.

Mindful Listening: Practice active listening in your interactions with others, giving them your full attention without interrupting or thinking ahead to your response. Notice the tone of their voice, their body language, and the emotions underlying their words. By listening mindfully, you can deepen your connections and foster empathy and understanding.

The Benefits of Mindfulness

The practice of mindfulness offers a myriad of benefits for our emotional and mental well-being:

Reduced Stress and Anxiety: Mindfulness has been shown to lower levels of cortisol, the stress hormone, and alleviate symptoms of anxiety and depression. By cultivating a sense of calm and relaxation, mindfulness can help us navigate life's challenges with greater resilience and ease.

Improved Focus and Concentration: By training our attention to stay anchored in the present moment, mindfulness strengthens our ability to concentrate and stay focused on the task at hand. This can enhance productivity, creativity, and performance in various areas of our lives.

Enhanced Emotional Regulation: Mindfulness helps us develop greater awareness of our thoughts and emotions, allowing us to respond to them with clarity and equanimity rather than reacting impulsively. This can lead to healthier relationships, improved communication, and a greater sense of emotional balance.

Greater Self-Compassion: Mindfulness encourages us to treat ourselves with kindness, compassion, and acceptance, even in the face of difficulties or setbacks. By cultivating a nonjudgmental attitude towards ourselves and our experiences, we can foster a deeper sense of self-love and acceptance.

Incorporating Meditation into Your Practice

In addition to mindfulness, meditation is another powerful tool for fostering emotional and mental wellness. Meditation involves intentionally directing our attention inward, often through techniques such as focused attention, loving-kindness, or body awareness.

Here are some simple meditation practices you can try:

Focused Attention Meditation: Choose a focal point for your attention, such as your breath, a mantra, or a visual object. Whenever your mind wanders, gently bring it back to your chosen focal point, without judgment or frustration.

Loving-Kindness Meditation: Cultivate feelings of love, compassion, and goodwill towards yourself and others by silently repeating phrases such as "May I be happy, may I be healthy, may I be at peace." Expand these wishes to include loved ones, acquaintances, and even people you may have difficulty with.

Body Scan Meditation: Bring your attention to different parts of your body, starting from your toes and moving up to your head. Notice any sensations, tension, or discomfort, and allow yourself to relax and release any areas of tension you may encounter.

Guided Visualization: Listen to a guided meditation that leads you through a visualization exercise, such as imagining yourself in a peaceful natural setting or visualizing positive outcomes for your goals and aspirations.

By incorporating meditation into your mindfulness practice, you can deepen your self-awareness, cultivate inner peace, and.

Enhancing Emotional Intelligence

Emotional intelligence, often referred to as EQ, encompasses our ability to understand, manage, and express our emotions effectively. By enhancing our emotional intelligence, we can cultivate greater resilience, build stronger relationships, and navigate life's challenges with grace and wisdom.

Understanding Emotional Intelligence

Emotional intelligence is like a compass that guides us through the ups and downs of life. It involves being aware of our own emotions and those of others, recognizing how our emotions influence our thoughts and behaviors, and effectively managing our emotions in various situations. Unlike IQ, which measures cognitive abilities, EQ focuses on our ability to perceive, understand, and regulate emotions—a skill that is essential for success and well-being in all areas of life.

The Importance of Emotional Intelligence

Emotional intelligence plays a crucial role in our mental and emotional health, influencing how we navigate relationships, handle stress, and cope with adversity. Research has shown that individuals with higher levels of emotional intelligence are more likely to experience greater happiness, lower levels of stress, and stronger social connections. They are better equipped to communicate effectively, resolve conflicts peacefully, and bounce back from setbacks with resilience.

Practical Strategies for Enhancing Emotional Intelligence

Self-Awareness: Start by cultivating self-awareness—the foundation of emotional intelligence. Take time to reflect on your thoughts, feelings, and reactions to different situations. Pay attention to your body's signals and notice how your emotions manifest physically. Journaling, meditation, and mindfulness practices can help deepen your self-awareness and enhance your emotional intelligence.

Self-Regulation: Learn to regulate your emotions by developing healthy coping strategies and stress management techniques. Practice relaxation techniques such as deep breathing, progressive muscle relaxation, or yoga to calm your mind and body during times of stress. Cultivate resilience by reframing negative thoughts, practicing gratitude, and focusing on solutions rather than dwelling on problems.

Empathy: Cultivate empathy—the ability to understand and share the feelings of others. Practice active listening, seek to understand others' perspectives, and validate their emotions without judgment. Empathy fosters deeper connections and strengthens relationships, contributing to your overall emotional intelligence.

Social Skills: Develop your social skills by honing your communication, conflict resolution, and interpersonal skills. Practice assertive communication, express yourself clearly and respectfully, and actively listen to others' viewpoints. Build rapport with others, collaborate effectively, and navigate social dynamics with confidence and ease.

Mindfulness: Incorporate mindfulness practices into your daily routine to cultivate present-moment awareness and emotional resilience. Engage in activities such as meditation, mindful breathing, or body scan exercises to anchor yourself in the present moment and reduce stress. Mindfulness enhances self-awareness, self-regulation, and overall emotional intelligence.

By incorporating these practical strategies into your life, you can enhance your emotional intelligence and foster greater emotional and mental wellness. Emotional intelligence is a skill that can be developed and refined over time with practice and persistence.

Strategies for Coping with Challenges

Life is filled with ups and downs, twists and turns, and unexpected challenges that can leave us feeling overwhelmed, stressed, and uncertain. In times of adversity, it's essential to have strategies in place to cope with challenges and foster emotional and mental wellness. By equipping ourselves with effective coping mechanisms, we can navigate life's hurdles with resilience, strength, and grace.

Practice Self-Compassion:

One of the most powerful tools for coping with challenges is practicing self-compassion. Instead of being hard on yourself or engaging in negative self-talk, treat yourself with kindness, understanding, and acceptance. Remember that it's okay to struggle, and that you are worthy of love and compassion, no matter what challenges you may face.

Cultivate Gratitude:

In moments of difficulty, it can be easy to focus on the negative aspects of our lives. However, cultivating gratitude can help shift our perspective and remind us of the blessings that surround us. Take time each day to reflect on the things you are grateful for, whether it's a supportive friend, a beautiful sunset, or a moment of peace and quiet.

Seek Support:

During challenging times, it's important to reach out for support from trusted friends, family members, or mental health professionals. Don't hesitate to lean on your support network for guidance, encouragement, and reassurance. Remember that you don't have to face challenges alone, and that there are people who care about you and want to help.

Practice Mindfulness:

Mindfulness is a powerful practice for coping with challenges and fostering emotional and mental wellness. By staying present in the moment and observing your thoughts and feelings without judgment, you can cultivate a sense of calm, clarity, and inner peace. Take time each day to practice mindfulness through activities such as meditation, deep breathing, or simply being present in nature.

Set Realistic Expectations:

When facing challenges, it's important to set realistic expectations for yourself and others. Avoid putting unnecessary pressure on yourself to achieve perfection or to have all the answers. Instead, focus on making progress one step at a time, and celebrate small victories along the way.

Practice Self-Care:

Self-care is essential for maintaining emotional and mental wellness, especially during challenging times. Make time each day to prioritize activities that nourish your mind, body, and soul, whether it's taking a warm bath, going for a walk, or indulging in a hobby you love. Remember that self-care is not selfish—it's essential for your overall well-being.

Develop Healthy Coping Skills:

Instead of turning to unhealthy coping mechanisms such as substance abuse or avoidance, focus on developing healthy coping skills that help you navigate challenges in a positive and constructive way. This may include journaling, exercising, practicing relaxation techniques, or seeking professional help when needed.

Practice Resilience:

Resilience is the ability to bounce back from adversity and emerge stronger than before. Cultivate resilience by reframing challenges as opportunities for growth, learning from setbacks, and maintaining a positive outlook, even in the face of adversity. Remember that challenges are temporary, but your resilience is enduring.

In conclusion, coping with challenges and fostering emotional and mental wellness requires practice, patience, and perseverance. By incorporating these strategies into your daily life, you can build resilience, cultivate inner peace, and navigate life's challenges with grace and strength.

Sustaining Healthy Habits for the Long Term

In our journey towards maintaining healthy habits for the long term, we're bound to encounter challenges such as plateaus and setbacks. These obstacles can feel disheartening, but they're a natural part of the process. Here, we'll explore strategies for overcoming these hurdles and continuing on our path to wellness.

Understanding Plateaus

Plateaus are periods where we stop seeing progress despite our best efforts. Whether it's weight loss, fitness gains, or other health goals, plateaus can leave us feeling frustrated and demotivated. However, it's essential to remember that plateaus are normal and can happen to anyone.

Tips for Overcoming Plateaus

Reevaluate Your Goals: Take a step back and reassess your goals. Are they still relevant and achievable? Adjusting your goals can help reignite your motivation and focus.

Mix Up Your Routine: Plateaus often occur when our bodies become accustomed to our exercise or diet regimen. Try switching things up by trying new exercises, changing your workout routine, or experimenting with different healthy foods.

Stay Consistent: Consistency is key to overcoming plateaus. Stick to your healthy habits, even when progress seems slow. Remember that small, consistent efforts add up over time.

Monitor Your Progress: Keep track of your progress using metrics like measurements, fitness assessments, or food journals. While it's essential not to obsess over numbers, monitoring your progress can help you identify areas for improvement and celebrate small victories along the way.

Stay Positive: Plateaus can be frustrating, but maintaining a positive mindset is crucial. Focus on how far you've come and the positive changes you've made in your life. Remember that setbacks are temporary, and with persistence, you'll overcome them.

Dealing with Setbacks: Setbacks are inevitable on the journey to long-term health and wellness. Whether it's a missed workout, a slip-up in your diet, or a temporary lapse in motivation, setbacks are a natural part of the process. Here's how to bounce back when setbacks occur:

Practice Self-Compassion: Be kind to yourself when setbacks happen. Instead of beating yourself up, acknowledge your feelings, and remind yourself that setbacks are an opportunity for growth and learning.

Learn from Mistakes: Reflect on what led to the setback and identify any patterns or triggers that contributed to it. Use setbacks as a learning opportunity to make adjustments and develop strategies for avoiding similar pitfalls in the future.

Focus on Solutions: Instead of dwelling on the setback, shift your focus to finding solutions. What steps can you take to get back on track? Whether it's scheduling extra workouts, meal prepping healthy meals, or seeking support from a friend or coach, take proactive steps to move forward.

Stay Flexible: Recognize that setbacks are a normal part of the journey and that progress is rarely linear. Be flexible and adaptable, adjusting your approach as needed to overcome obstacles and stay on course towards your goals.

Celebrate Progress: Even in the face of setbacks, celebrate the progress you've made so far. Remember that setbacks don't erase your achievements or define your journey. Every step forward, no matter how small, brings you closer to your goals.

Overcoming plateaus and setbacks is a vital aspect of sustaining healthy habits for the long term. Setbacks are temporary, and with perseverance and determination, you can overcome them and emerge stronger than ever.

Building Resilience and Adaptability

Life is full of ups and downs, and challenges are inevitable. But by cultivating resilience and adaptability, we can navigate these challenges with grace and emerge stronger than ever before. Resilience is the ability to bounce back from adversity, to withstand setbacks, and to thrive in the face of challenges. It's like a muscle that can be strengthened with practice and perseverance. When we encounter obstacles on our path to healthy living—whether it's a setback in our fitness journey, a temptation to indulge in unhealthy foods, or a stressful life event—resilience allows us to stay focused on our goals, pick ourselves up, and keep moving forward.

So, how can we build resilience in our lives? Here are some practical strategies to help you cultivate resilience and adaptability:

Cultivate a Positive Mindset: Adopting a positive mindset can help you view challenges as opportunities for growth and learning. Instead of dwelling on setbacks, focus on the lessons you can learn from them and the ways in which they can make you stronger.

Practice Self-Compassion: Treat yourself with kindness and compassion, especially during difficult times. Remember that it's okay to stumble along the way—what matters is how you respond to those setbacks. Offer yourself words of encouragement and support, just as you would to a dear friend.

Build a Support Network: Surround yourself with people who uplift and support you on your journey to wellness. Whether it's friends, family members, or a supportive community, having a strong support network can provide you with the encouragement and guidance you need to overcome challenges.

Develop Coping Skills: Equip yourself with healthy coping mechanisms to deal with stress and adversity. Practice relaxation techniques such as deep breathing, meditation, or yoga to help you stay centered and calm in the face of life's challenges.

Set Realistic Goals: Break down your health and wellness goals into manageable steps, and celebrate your progress along the way. Setting realistic expectations for yourself can help prevent feelings of overwhelm and increase your confidence in your ability to succeed.

Stay Flexible: Life is unpredictable, and it's essential to remain flexible and adaptable in the face of change. Be willing to adjust your plans and strategies as needed, and embrace the opportunities that come your way, even if they deviate from your original path.

Practice Gratitude: Cultivate an attitude of gratitude by focusing on the positive aspects of your life, even during challenging times. Keeping a gratitude journal or simply taking a few moments each day to reflect on the things you're thankful for can help shift your perspective and boost your resilience.

Learn from Failure: Instead of viewing failure as a sign of weakness, see it as an opportunity for growth and self-improvement. Reflect on your experiences, identify what went wrong, and use those insights to inform your future actions.

Resilience is not about avoiding challenges or hardships—it's about facing them head-on with courage, strength, and determination. With resilience and adaptability by your side, there's no obstacle too great to overcome on your path to lifelong wellness.

Staying Consistent and Persistent

When it comes to sustaining healthy habits for the long term, consistency and persistence are key. While starting a new habit can be exciting and motivating, sticking with it over time requires dedication, commitment, and a willingness to persevere through challenges.

Set Realistic Expectations: One of the most important aspects of staying consistent and persistent is setting realistic expectations for yourself. Understand that progress takes time and that setbacks are a natural part of the process. Instead of aiming for perfection, focus on making small, sustainable changes that you can maintain over the long term.

Establish a Routine: Creating a consistent routine can help reinforce healthy habits and make them feel more automatic. Set specific times each day for exercise, meal prep, mindfulness practice, and other health-related activities. By incorporating these habits into your daily schedule, you'll be more likely to stick with them over time.

Track Your Progress: Monitoring your progress can help keep you motivated and accountable. Keep track of your workouts, meals, mood, and other relevant metrics using a journal, app, or tracker. Celebrate your successes, no matter how small, and use setbacks as opportunities for learning and growth.

Find Accountability: Having a support system in place can greatly increase your chances of staying consistent with your healthy habits. Find a workout buddy, join a support group, or enlist the help of a coach or mentor who can hold you accountable and provide encouragement along the way.

Focus on the Why: Remind yourself of why you started your healthy habits in the first place. Whether it's to improve your health, boost your energy levels, or feel more confident in your own skin, keeping your goals front and center can help you stay motivated during challenging times.

Practice Self-Compassion: Be kind to yourself, especially when things don't go as planned. Remember that setbacks are a normal part of the process and that you're only human. Instead of dwelling on your mistakes, focus on what you can learn from them and how you can adjust your approach moving forward.

Stay Flexible: Life is unpredictable, and there will inevitably be times when your routine gets disrupted. Instead of letting these disruptions derail your progress, stay flexible and find alternative ways to stay on track. Whether it's squeezing in a quick workout during your lunch break or making healthier choices when dining out, adaptability is key to long-term success.

Seek Support When Needed: Don't be afraid to reach out for support when you need it. Whether you're struggling with motivation, facing a plateau, or feeling overwhelmed, there are people who can help you navigate through the challenges. Reach out to friends, family members, or professionals who can offer guidance, encouragement, and support along the way.

By staying consistent and persistent in your efforts, you can overcome obstacles, break through barriers, and achieve your health and wellness goals. Every step forward, no matter how small, brings you closer to the vibrant, healthy life you deserve. So keep moving forward, stay focused on your goals, and never underestimate the power of consistency and persistence in creating lasting change.

Creating a Supportive Environment

When it comes to sustaining healthy habits for the long term, creating a supportive environment is key. Your surroundings can have a significant impact on your behavior, making it easier—or harder—to stick to your goals. By intentionally designing your environment to support your health and well-being, you can set yourself up for success and make it easier to maintain your healthy habits over time.

Clear Out Temptations: Start by decluttering your space and removing any temptations that may derail your progress. Get rid of unhealthy snacks, sugary treats, and other trigger foods that may tempt you to veer off course. Replace them with nourishing options that align with your health goals.

Stock Up on Healthy Options: Fill your pantry, fridge, and countertops with nutritious foods that support your health and well-being. Stock up on fresh fruits and vegetables, lean proteins, whole grains, and other wholesome ingredients that make it easy to prepare healthy meals and snacks. Make Healthy Choices Visible and Accessible: Keep healthy foods front and center in your kitchen, making them the first thing you see when you open the fridge or pantry. Store pre-cut fruits and veggies in clear containers at eye level, making them easy to grab and go when hunger strikes.

Create a Meal Prep Station: Designate a specific area in your kitchen for meal prep, making it easier to prepare healthy meals in advance. Invest in quality storage containers, chopping boards, and kitchen gadgets to streamline the process and save time during busy weekdays.

Set Up a Home Gym or Workout Space: Create a dedicated workout space in your home, whether it's a corner of your living room, a spare bedroom, or even just a yoga mat in your backyard. Having a designated space for exercise makes it easier to stay active and prioritize movement each day.

Surround Yourself with Supportive People: Surround yourself with friends, family members, and coworkers who share your commitment to health and wellness. Seek out like-minded individuals who can offer encouragement, accountability, and support as you work towards your goals.

Communicate Your Needs: Don't be afraid to communicate your health goals and needs to those around you. Let your friends and family know how they can support you on your journey, whether it's by joining you for workouts, cooking healthy meals together, or offering words of encouragement when you need them most.

Limit Exposure to Negative Influences: Be mindful of the media you consume, including social media, news outlets, and other sources of information. Limit your exposure to negative influences that may undermine your confidence or trigger unhealthy behaviors, and instead focus on sources of inspiration and positivity that uplift and motivate you.

Create a Relaxing Environment: Designate a space in your home where you can unwind and relax after a long day. Whether it's a cozy reading nook, a soothing bath, or a meditation corner, having a peaceful retreat where you can de-stress and recharge is essential for maintaining your overall well-being.

Practice Self-Compassion: Finally, remember to be kind to yourself as you navigate your health journey. Embrace imperfection, celebrate progress, and treat yourself with the same compassion and understanding that you would offer to a loved one. Building healthy habits takes time and effort, so be patient with yourself and trust in your ability to create a supportive environment that fosters your growth and well-being.

Small changes can add up to big results over time, so focus on making gradual improvements and building momentum as you work towards your health and wellness goals. With the right environment and mindset, you can achieve lasting transformation and live your best life.

*Please can for the other books of the **"Life Mastery"** Series.*

www.ingramcontent.com/pod-product-compliance
Lightning Source LLC
Chambersburg PA
CBHW070346230526
45471CB00006B/2435